MW01594927

COSTA BRAVA TRAVEL GUIDE
2023 - 2024

A Comprehensive Tourist Guide To Costa Brava: Discovering The Gems And Vibrant History of Catalan Coastline Wth Complete Essential Tips & 7 Days Itinerary

BY

William Jose

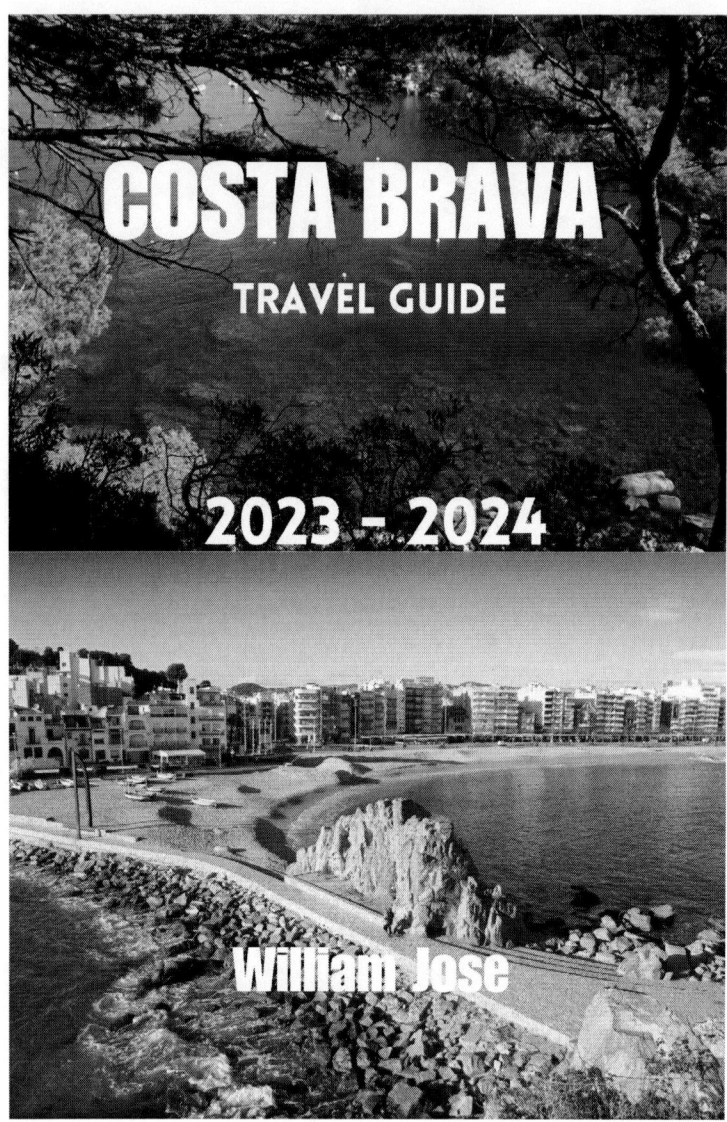

COSTA BRAVA
TRAVEL GUIDE

2023 - 2024

William Jose

TABLE OF CONTENTS

<u>INTRODUCTION</u>

Costa Brava, known as "Wild Coast" in Catalan, is a gorgeous coastal landscape in northeastern Spain that stretches from Blanes to the French border. Costa Brava, known for its stunning landscapes, quaint towns, pristine beaches, and crystal-clear seas, has become a popular tourist destination for those seeking a combination of natural beauty, cultural legacy, and Mediterranean charm.

The coastline of the area stretches for around 214 kilometers (133 miles), covering a broad variety of scenery such as rocky cliffs, quiet coves, and sandy beaches. These magnificent coastline rocks have long inspired painters and authors, and their stunning beauty continues to enchant tourists.

The many fishing villages and tourist towns that dot the Costa Brava coastline are one of its most distinguishing characteristics. Cadaqués, Tossa de Mar, Begur, and Roses have a distinct attractiveness due to its whitewashed buildings, small alleyways, and gorgeous ports. With historic ruins, medieval strongholds, and lovely old neighborhoods that represent the region's cultural heritage, these towns provide an insight into the region's rich past.

Costa Brava has a diversified natural environment in addition to its coastline attractiveness. Several environmental reserves, notably the Cap de Creus Natural Park and the Aiguamolls de l'Empordà Natural Park, are located in the area, where tourists may explore unspoiled landscapes, stroll along picturesque routes, and see a diversity of plant and animal species.

Costa Brava has a thriving culinary industry, with a focus on fresh seafood, locally produced products, and traditional Catalan cuisine. Paella, fideuà (a seafood-based meal similar to paella but with noodles), and de (a fish stew) are among the delectable foods available to visitors. Costa Brava has a variety of activities for outdoor enthusiasts, including swimming, snorkeling, scuba diving, sailing, and kayaking. The pleasant Mediterranean environment of the area, with sunny summers and mild winters, making it a perfect destination for both beachgoers and outdoor enthusiasts.

Costa Brava provides a fascinating experience that blends breathtaking landscapes, rich history, and a dynamic cultural scene, whether you're looking for leisure on the beach, visiting attractive coastal villages, or immersing yourself in natural beauty.

Brief History of Costa Brava

The Costa Brava is a coastal area in northeastern Catalonia, Spain. It translates to "Wild Coast" or "Rough Coast" in English. It extends from Blanes, approximately 60 kilometers (37 miles) northeast of Barcelona, to the French border.

The history of the Costa Brava is inextricably linked to the history of Catalonia. The area has been populated from prehistoric times, with evidence of Paleolithic human habitation. Various civilizations, including the Iberians, Romans, Visigoths, and Moors, have left their imprint on the Costa Brava throughout the years.

The Costa Brava was part of Hispania Tarraconensis during the Roman era. The Romans created several towns and advanced agriculture, commerce, and infrastructure throughout the area. They constructed roads, bridges, and villas, some of which may still be viewed today, such as the Empire's ruins.

The Costa Brava witnessed political and geographical fragmentation in the early medieval era. It was controlled by a number of local lords and counts, notably the Counties of

Empires and Barcelona. As many nations vied for supremacy, the area experienced its fair share of wars and skirmishes.

Several fortifications and castles were built along the shore throughout the medieval period to defend against pirates and invaders. Tossa de Mar and Palamós are well-known for their well-preserved medieval walls and defenses.

The Costa Brava saw substantial alterations over the twentieth century. The area started to attract artists, philosophers, and authors in the early twentieth century, attracted to its natural beauty and unusual sceneries. The Costa Brava has influenced artists such as Salvador Dal, Pablo Picasso, and Joan Miró.

The Costa Brava underwent a tourist boom in the 1950s and 1960s, with the building of infrastructure, hotels, and resorts. This resulted in an inflow of tourists, particularly from Northern Europe, looking for sun, sand, and sea. While tourism has provided economic advantages to the area, it has also presented issues in terms of environmental preservation and balancing growth with conservation.

The Costa Brava is still a popular tourist destination today, thanks to its scenic coastal villages, stunning beaches, craggy cliffs, and crystal-clear seas. It has a diverse range of historical and cultural sites, outdoor activities, and a thriving culinary scene, making it a popular holiday destination for visitors from all over the globe.

Costa Brava population

The Costa Brava region's population is believed to be over 1.7 million people. The area is well-known for its stunning beaches, charming coastal villages, and rich cultural legacy. Due to its natural beauty, historical landmarks, and Mediterranean temperature, it draws a large number of visitors, particularly during the summer months. Costa Brava's population has most certainly grown since then, but for the most up-to-date and accurate population data, it is best to consult official sources such as government publications, statistical reports, or municipal authorities.

Costa Brava Religion Practice

Costa Brava, on Spain's northeastern coast, is recognized for its beautiful beaches, charming villages, and lively culture. In terms of religion, Costa Brava represents Spain's primary religious views and customs.

Roman Catholicism is the major religion in Costa Brava, as it is across Spain. The area has a strong history of Catholicism and is home to many spectacular churches, cathedrals, and religious monuments. Catholicism is important in many inhabitants' lives, with frequent church attendance and involvement in religious festivals and rituals.

Along with Catholicism, other religious faiths are becoming more prevalent in Costa Brava. In recent years, Protestantism, particularly diverse evangelical and charismatic groups, has grown in popularity. There are also communities of Muslims, Jews, and other religious minorities, reflecting the region's multiculturalism.

In Costa Brava, religious traditions include a wide range of ceremonies and festivities. Traditional Catholic norms govern the conduct of Catholic mass, baptisms, marriages, and funerals. Religious holidays such as Christmas and Easter are also celebrated with zeal throughout the area, with processions, feasts, and religious rituals.

Spiritual tourism and other types of spirituality have also increased in Costa Brava in recent years. Yoga retreats, meditation institutes, and health practices have grown in popularity among both residents and tourists, providing a unique perspective on spirituality and personal development.

Overall, religion in Costa Brava is predominantly based on Roman Catholicism, although the area also values religious pluralism, as seen by the existence of various religions and alternative spiritual practices.

Chapter One

Navigating the Costa Brava, Spanish Tourist Heaven

Costa Brava is a place where adventure meets the glistening Mediterranean. Travel through picturesque coastal communities, take in the sun-kissed beaches, and experience the lively culture on a vacation that will awaken your senses. Allow the thrill of discovery to lead your feet as you discover the hidden treasures this wonderful area has to offer. Costa Brava crafts a tapestry of excitement with each new discovery, tempting you to immerse yourself in its beauty and create memories that will eternally dance in your heart.

Air Travel To Costa Brava

Travel to Costa Brava, a seaside area in northern Spain, is made easier by the closeness of many airports. Barcelona-El Prat Airport (BCN) and Girona-Costa Brava Airport (GRO) are the two primary airports servicing the area. Flight availability and prices may vary based on your departure location. Here is some information on flying to Costa Brava from several locations:

From within Spain:

Barcelona-El Prat Airport (BCN): If you are already in Spain, numerous flights to Barcelona-El Prat Airport are available. You may easily access Costa Brava by car or train from there. Flight prices vary depending on your departure city inside Spain and the time of year you book.

From the continent of Europe:

Several airlines operate direct flights from London to Barcelona-El Prat Airport or Girona-Costa Brava Airport. The flight lasts around 2-3 hours. The cost may vary based on the airline, the season, and how far in advance you book.

Paris, France: There are direct flights from Paris to Barcelona-El Prat Airport. The flight lasts around 1.5-2 hours. Again, pricing will vary depending on a variety of circumstances.

Frankfurt, Germany: Direct flights from Frankfurt to Barcelona-El Prat Airport are available on certain carriers. The flight lasts around 2-3 hours. Prices may vary depending on the airline and the terms of the ticket.

Outside of Europe:

New York City, United States: There are direct flights from New York to Barcelona-El Prat Airport. The flight lasts around 8-9 hours. The cost will vary according to the airline, season, and time of booking.

Toronto, Canada: There are direct flights from Toronto to Barcelona-El Prat Airport. Flight time is around 8-9 hours. Prices will vary according to the airline and other variables.

Flight availability and rates may fluctuate over time, so it's best to check with airlines or online travel agents for the most up-to-date information. When booking your flight to Costa Brava, keep in mind things like luggage limitations, layovers, and probable visa needs.

Land Travel To Costa Brava

The cost and availability of land travel to Costa Brava varies depending on your starting point. The following are some popular starting sites and ways of transportation:

Barcelona (Spain)

By vehicle: The most convenient way is to hire a vehicle in Barcelona and travel to Costa Brava. Depending on your location along the coast, the trip takes roughly 1.5 to 2 hours.

By Bus: There are many bus companies that run frequent trips between Barcelona and villages along the Costa Brava.

The price varies, but a one-way ticket should cost between €10 and €20 ($12-$24).

Girona is a city in Spain.

By vehicle: Girona is a key regional transportation center, and hiring a vehicle is a popular way to explore Costa Brava. Driving time from Girona to other seaside towns ranges from 20 minutes to 1 hour.

By rail: Girona has great rail links, and you can take a train to any of the cities along the Costa Brava. Train rates vary depending on the location, but a one-way ticket should cost between €5 and €15 ($6-$18).

By Bus: Similar to Barcelona, frequent bus services run from Girona to other cities along the Costa Brava. The one-way ticket rates are similar, ranging from €10 to €20 ($12-$24). Barcelona (El Prat) Airport, Spain:

Renting a vehicle from Barcelona Airport is an easy alternative. Driving time to Costa Brava varies depending on your destination and might vary from 1.5 to 2.5 hours.

By Bus: Direct bus services are available from Barcelona Airport to numerous communities along the Costa Brava.

The ticket rates are comparable to those from Barcelona's city center, ranging between €10 and €20 ($12 and $24) for a one-way ride.

Costa Brava Sea Travel

Costa Brava is a lovely coastal area in northeastern Spain noted for its magnificent beaches, picturesque coastal villages, and crystal-clear seas. If you want to go to Costa Brava by water, your alternatives may differ based on your starting point. Here are some broad alternatives and estimated expenses for maritime transport to Costa Brava from various points:

Barcelona, Spain: A frequent starting place for visitors to Costa Brava is Barcelona. Ferries run from Barcelona's Port Vell to several places along the Costa Brava coastline, including Blanes, Lloret de Mar, and Tossa de Mar. The fares may vary from €10 and €25 per person, depending on the location and the operator.

Marseille, France: If you're traveling from Marseille, France, you may take a boat to Barcelona and then use the alternatives listed above to continue your trip to Costa Brava. The boat ride from Marseille to Barcelona takes around 8-10 hours, and the cost varies based on the ferry company and the kind of cabin or seat you choose. For a one-way journey, rates typically range between €50 and €100 per person.

Palma de Mallorca, Spain: Palma de Mallorca is a Balearic Sea island with links to various Costa Brava locations. You may take a ferry from Palma de Mallorca to places on the Costa Brava such as Roses or Palamós. boat rates may vary from €50 to €100 per person, depending on the boat company and the kind of cabin or seat you choose.

Ibiza, Spain: Another popular starting place for visitors to Costa Brava is Ibiza. You may take a boat from Ibiza to Barcelona and then use the previously listed methods to continue your travel to Costa Brava. Ferry rates from Ibiza to Barcelona are identical to those described above, with one-way tickets beginning from €50-€100.

Please keep in mind that the costs shown are estimates and may change based on variables such as the time of year, availability, and the boat operator. It is usually best to check with ferry operators or travel agents for the most up-to-date timetables and rates.

Best Time To Visit Costa Brava

The months of May through September are ideal for visiting Costa Brava, a magnificent seaside area in northeastern Spain. Warm and pleasant weather prevails throughout these months, making them excellent for outdoor activities and seeing the region's stunning beaches and lovely villages.

The summer months of June to August are the busiest for tourists on the Costa Brava. The beaches are lively, and the sea is ideal for swimming and other water sports. This is also the season for numerous festivals and events, which provide a dynamic and bustling environment.

If you like to avoid crowds, traveling in May or September is an excellent choice. The weather is still great, and there are less visitors to appreciate the region's splendor. During these months, the water is often warm enough for swimming.

Overall, the best time to visit Costa Brava for the complete experience is during the summer months, but if you want a calmer stay, May or September are excellent.

Month by Month Weather in Costa Brava

Costa Brava is a coastal area in northeastern Spain famed for its attractive communities, lovely beaches, and warm Mediterranean climate. Here's a look at the weather in Costa Brava month by month:

January:

Temperature: 8°C (46°F) on average

Rainfall: 39 millimeters

The coldest month in Costa Brava is January, with chilly temperatures and considerable rain. Although it is not perfect for beach activities, the area is less congested, and you may tour the cities and enjoy interior attractions.

February:

Temperature: 9°C (48°F) on average

Rainfall: 33 millimeters

February, like January, is rather chilly with intermittent rain. Although it is still considered the off-season, you may benefit from reduced accommodation prices and fewer people.

March:

Temperature: 11°C (52°F) on average

Rainfall: 36 millimeters

In March, spring arrives, and temperatures begin to increase. It's still a little cold, but you could have some nice sunny days. It's a great time for trekking and discovering Costa Brava's natural splendor.

April:

Temperature: 13°C (55°F) on average

Rainfall: 39 millimeters

Temperatures rise higher in April, making the weather more pleasant. If you prefer warmer weather and wish to escape the summer crowds, this is a fantastic time to come.

May:

Temperature: 16°C (61°F) on average

Total rainfall: 49mm

May offers higher temperatures and the pinnacle of the spring blossoms. It's a great time to visit Costa Brava since the weather is nice and the water is warming up.

June:

Temperature: 20°C (68°F) on average

Rainfall: 34 millimeters

The summer season in Costa Brava officially begins in June. The weather is nice, and the beaches are becoming more crowded. Water sports and outdoor activities are popular at this time of year.

July:

Temperature: 23°C (73°F) on average

Rainfall total: 28mm

July is one of the warmest months on the Costa Brava, with high temperatures and lots of sunlight. It's peak tourist season, so the beaches are busy. Swimming and sunbathing are both popular pastimes.

August:

Temperature: 24°C (75°F) on average

32mm rainfall

August is another hot and crowded month on the Costa Brava. The weather is hot, and the sea is warm. It's a fantastic time to visit the beach, but anticipate greater crowds and higher expenses.

September

Temperature: 21°C (70°F) on average

Rainfall: 70 millimeters

September in Costa Brava is still warm, but somewhat colder than July and August. The water is still warm enough for swimming, and now is an excellent time to go if you want less people.

October:
Temperature: 17°C (63°F) on average
Rainfall: 77 millimeters
In Costa Brava, October heralds the arrival of fall. Temperatures begin to plummet, and more rain falls. It's a more peaceful period, and you can take in the wonderful fall countryside.

November:
Temperature: 12°C (54°F) on average
Rainfall: 57 millimeters
In Costa Brava, November is a generally cold and wet month. It's the off-season, so there will be less visitors. It's a terrific time for indoor activities, museums, and historical exploration.

December:
Temperature: 9°C (48°F) on average
Rainfall: 47 millimeters

December is comparable to November in terms of chilly temperatures and rainfall. It's the off season, so you can enjoy the festivities.

Transportation Options For Touring Costa Brava

There are numerous forms of transportation available to suit your interests and budget while traveling Costa Brava.

Car Rental: Renting a car gives you the greatest freedom and flexibility to explore the area at your own speed. The cost of car rental in Costa Brava varies based on the vehicle type, rental term, and rental operator. A basic budget automobile will cost you roughly €30-€60 per day on average.

Public Transport: Costa Brava has a well-connected public transit infrastructure that includes buses and trains. Buses are the most prevalent means of transportation, with trips to a variety of coastal and interior sites. Bus costs normally vary from €2 and €10 per journey, depending on distance. Trains are another alternative, particularly for trips to major cities like Barcelona or Girona, with costs ranging from €10 to €15.

bicycle: The stunning landscapes of Costa Brava make it a perfect location for bicycle aficionados. Bicycles are available for hire in several cities and rental businesses, with costs ranging from €10 to €30 per day.

Boat Tours: Exploring the Costa Brava by boat enables you to explore secret bays and take in the scenery. Boat cruises and excursions are offered at various pricing ranges, with short trips beginning at roughly €20.

Walking: Costa Brava has a number of hiking routes that enable you to explore the region's natural beauty on foot. Walking tours are often self-guided or conducted by expert guides, with prices ranging according to time and route.

It's crucial to remember that these prices are estimates that might change based on the season, demand, and particular suppliers. When renting a vehicle, you need also consider gasoline prices, parking fees, and tolls.

Chapter Two

Costa Brava Travel Preparation

Prepare to be enchanted by Costa Brava's magnificent splendor, where the sun kisses the crystal-clear seas and the craggy shoreline calls for adventure. Explore picturesque seaside towns, enjoy wonderful food, and immerse yourself in the rich history and culture of Catalonia. Pack your sense of wonder, appetite for adventure, and camera, for Costa Brava will leave an everlasting impact on your heart and spirit.

City Tour of Costa Brava's Neighborhoods

Costa Brava is a lovely coastal area in northern Spain famed for its magnificent beaches, steep cliffs, and quaint villages. Several neighborhoods and villages along the Costa Brava provide one-of-a-kind experiences and attractions. Here are a few prominent neighborhoods and towns to visit:

Cadaqués: Located on the Costa Brava's easternmost point, Cadaqués is a charming fishing community famed for its whitewashed buildings and tiny alleyways. It was formerly home to the famed artist Salvador Dal, and you can now visit his old mansion, which has been converted into a museum named Casa-Museu Salvador Dal. Cadaqués is ideal for a leisurely walk along the waterfront and dining on delicious seafood at one of the town's restaurants.

Tossa de Mar is a medieval town with a historic old section surrounded by ancient walls. The town is well-known for its lovely sandy beaches, particularly the major beach, Platja Gran, as well as the picturesque coastline views from the Vila Vella (Old Town). The majestic Tossa de Mar Castle, which gives panoramic views of the town and the Mediterranean Sea, should not be missed.

Lloret de Mar is a prominent resort town noted for its active nightlife and vast sandy beaches. It's a popular tourist area with a plethora of pubs, clubs, and restaurants. Aside from the bustling environment, historical places such as the Santa Clotilde Gardens, a magnificent park with breathtaking views of the sea, may be visited.

Begur: Perched on a hilltop, Begur combines medieval beauty with stunning seaside scenery. The town is distinguished for its tiny alleys, old structures, and a ruined castle. There are numerous gorgeous coves and beaches nearby, including Aiguablava, Sa Tuna, and Sa Riera, that are ideal for sunbathing and swimming.

Blanes: The "Gateway to the Costa Brava" is a famous summer getaway. The town has a lively waterfront promenade, lovely botanical gardens (Marimurtra and Pinya de Rosa), and extensive sandy beaches. Blanes also organizes the yearly International Fireworks Competition, which draws tourists from all around the globe.

Transit Options of Exploring the Neighborhoods

Costa Brava is a lovely coastal area in northeastern Spain recognized for its magnificent beaches, picturesque villages, and rich cultural history. Exploring the neighboring cities in Costa Brava may be a thrilling adventure. Here are some transportation alternatives and estimated prices for traveling about the neighborhood:

Bus: Buses are an easy and inexpensive method to travel between cities in Costa Brava. Several firms, notably Sarfa and Moventis, run a comprehensive bus network in the area.

A bus ticket between nearby cities normally costs between €2 and €10, depending on the distance traveled.

Rail: The Costa Brava rail network is well-developed, with quick links between major cities and communities. Renfe is Spain's national railway operator, and its regional routes include the Costa Brava area. Train rates might vary depending on distance and train type (regional, high-speed, etc.). Train tickets between adjacent cities might cost anything from €5 to €20 on average.

Car rental: Renting a car allows you to explore the Costa Brava area at your leisure. There are many vehicle rental companies in the region, and costs vary based on the rental time, automobile type, and rental business. Car rentals in Spain typically start about €20 per day, excluding gasoline and any insurance expenses.

Bicycle: The Costa Brava area is great for cycling lovers because of its mild temperature and picturesque scenery. Many cities in the vicinity hire bicycles, enabling you to explore the areas at your leisure. Bicycle rentals may vary from €10 to €30 per day.

Strolling: If you're staying in a certain city or town, strolling is a wonderful method to see the surrounding area. The seaside communities of Costa Brava often feature tiny city cores that are simple to traverse on foot. Walking is inexpensive and helps you to get immersed in the local culture.

It's crucial to remember that the prices shown above are estimates depending on the time of year, demand, and any special deals or discounts that may be available at the time this handbook was produced. Before making any trip arrangements, verify the current pricing and timetables with the relevant transit providers or rental companies.

What To Do In Costa Brava

Tourists may enjoy a variety of exciting activities on the Costa Brava. Costa Brava offers something for everyone, whether you prefer water activities, hiking, or exploring natural surroundings. Here are some fun things to do during your visit:

Scuba diving: Discover the beautiful underwater environment of Costa Brava. The shoreline is well-known for its clean waters and rich marine life, making it an ideal location for scuba diving. There are several diving facilities and schools that provide training and guided dives for both novice and expert divers.

Kayaking and stand-up paddleboarding Paddleboarding (SUP): Rent a kayak or a paddleboard and explore the coastline's stunning coves, caves, and cliffs. Paddle through the craggy terrain, exploring secret beaches and soaking in the gorgeous scenery.

Coasteering: Go on an amazing coasteering trip that includes rock climbing, cliff leaping, and swimming. You'll go down the shore with a guide, climbing cliffs, leaping into the water, and visiting sea caves. It's an exciting approach to appreciate Costa Brava's natural beauty.

Windsurfing and Kitesurfing: Take advantage of the Costa Brava's strong winds and try windsurfing or kitesurfing. The area provides ideal conditions for various water activities, and there are schools and rental businesses that provide equipment and courses to people of all skill levels.

Hiking the Camino de Ronda: The Camino de Ronda is a seaside trail that runs along the Costa Brava and offers breathtaking views of the Mediterranean Sea. There are many portions of the path to select from, ranging from simple walks to more difficult excursions. Explore the coastline on foot to see hidden beaches, cliffs, and quaint fishing communities.

Hot Air Balloon flight: Take a hot air balloon flight to see Costa Brava from a fresh viewpoint. Soar over the breathtaking scenery, which includes the coastline, rolling hills, and ancient villages. It's a one-of-a-kind, serene trip with breathtaking panoramic vistas.

Climbing: If you like rock climbing, Costa Brava has several climbing places with a variety of rock formations. There are climbs appropriate for all ability levels, from coastal cliffs to interior crags. Consider hiring a guide to secure your safety and to help you find the finest climbing areas.

Canyoning: Canyoning allows you to explore the interior gorges and canyons of Costa Brava. Descend waterfalls, leap into natural pools, and maneuver through tight spaces. It's a thrilling adventure that involves trekking, swimming, and rappelling.

Remember to check with local tour operators or tourist centers for availability, as well as any required permits or equipment for these activities. Stay safe and have a great time in Costa Brava!

Costa Brava Entry Requirements

If you want to visit Costa Brava as a tourist, the visa requirements may vary depending on your country and length of stay. The information below is usually applicable to residents of many countries, but it is essential to examine the exact visa requirements that apply to your place of residency.

Costa Brava is situated in Spain, which is a member of the Schengen Zone. You must apply for a Schengen visa if you are a citizen of a nation that is not excluded from the visa requirement. This visa permits you to visit Costa Brava and other Schengen countries for up to 90 days during a 180-day period.

Visa-exempt nations: For a short time, citizens of certain nations may visit Spain and the Schengen Area without a visa. Among these nations are the United States, Canada, Australia, New Zealand, Japan, South Korea, and the majority of European Union (EU) member states. Please keep in mind that the authorized duration of stay may vary.

Long-Term Visas: If you want to remain in Costa Brava for more than 90 days, you must apply for a long-term visa or residency permit. These visas are provided for a variety of reasons, including job, study, and family reunification. Depending on the purpose of your visit, the particular criteria and processes for long-term visas may change.

It's important to remember that visa requirements can change, so it's best to check with official sources like the Spanish embassy or consulate in your country or the Spanish Ministry of Foreign Affairs for the most up-to-date information on visa requirements for visiting Costa Brava.

Furthermore, bear in mind that visa requirements may vary depending on criteria such as the purpose of your journey, your financial means, and your previous travel history. It is best to plan your vacation well in advance and leave enough time for visa processing if necessary.

Where To Stay In Costa Brava

Costa Brava is a beautiful coastline area with wonderful villages. Here are some of the best tourist cities in Costa Brava to stay in:

Girona is a lively city with a rich history and a well-preserved medieval neighborhood. It has a stunning church, historic city walls, and winding cobblestone lanes. Girona also has great eating choices, cultural activities, including the Museum of Art.

Tossa de Mar is a coastal jewel with a beautiful beach and a picturesque ancient town. The historic stronghold with a view of the sea is a must-see, and the town's tiny alleys are lined with stores, restaurants, and cafés. Tossa de Mar is well-known for its laid-back ambiance and stunning seaside views.

Lloret de Mar is a renowned tourist destination noted for its busy nightlife, stunning beaches, and energetic environment. It has a variety of entertainment alternatives, such as water sports, beach bars, and clubs. Cultural features in Lloret de Mar include the Santa Clotilde Gardens.

Cadaqués is a lovely seaside town that has long served as a sanctuary for artists and authors. Its whitewashed cottages, small lanes, and beautiful harbor make it an appealing spot to visit. The town also has various art galleries and is well-known for its ties to Salvador Dal, who lived in neighboring Portlligat.

Begur: Begur is a medieval village on a mountaintop with stunning views of the coastline. Its old center has lovely architecture, such as a castle and tiny lanes packed with stores and restaurants. Begur is particularly well-known for its stunning beaches and pristine seas.

Roses: Roses is a seaside town with a vast sandy beach and a variety of water sports. It boasts a vibrant marina, a lovely old town, and an antique fortress. Roses is an excellent starting point for visiting the adjacent Cap de Creus Natural Park.

Blanes: Blanes is a beach town on the Costa Brava's southern tip. It has stunning beaches, a busy town center, and the lovely Marimurtra botanical park. The Concurs de Focs d'Artifici, an annual fireworks competition, is also held in Blanes.

These Costa Brava towns provide a variety of cultural, historical, and natural features, making them popular alternatives for visitors to the area.

Costa Brava Stay duration

The length of time you should stay in Costa Brava as a tourist depends on your tastes and the activities you wish to participate in. However, it is recommended that you spend 4 to 7 days exploring the area and enjoying its attractions. This time period enables you to enjoy the stunning coastline scenery, lovely towns and villages, relaxing on the beaches, and sampling the local food.

Costa Brava Packing Essentials

When preparing for a vacation to Costa Brava, there are a few basics to consider. Here's a packing list to get you started:

Clothing:
T-shirts, shorts, sundresses, and skirts that are lightweight and breathable.
Walking shoes that are comfortable: Sneakers or sandals for touring towns and trekking.

Swimsuit: Take advantage of the stunning beaches and seaside activities.

For chilly nights or unexpected weather changes, wear a light jacket or sweater.

Sunglasses and a hat provide UV protection.

In case of light rain, bring a rain jacket or an umbrella.

Travel accouterments include:

Charge your gadgets using a travel adaptor since plug types vary.

Portable charger: Keep your gadgets charged while you're on the road.

Toiletries in travel sizes: shampoo, conditioner, toothpaste, and so on.

Insect repellent: This is especially important if you want to spend time in rural regions.

Passport, ID, travel insurance, and any applicable visas are all required travel papers.

Cash and credit cards: Inform your bank of your trip arrangements.

Outdoor equipment:

Daypack: Perfect for treks and day outings.

Hiking boots or shoes: If you want to visit the region's natural parks.

Stay hydrated throughout your outdoor activities by carrying a water bottle.

Snorkeling equipment: Explore marine life in the clear seas.

Relax on the sandy beaches with a beach towel or mat.

Electronics:

Capture the breathtaking scenery and charming cities with your camera.

Smartphone: This device is useful for navigation, translation, and keeping connected.

E-reader or books: For entertainment or beach relaxation.

Headphones: Listen to music or podcasts while on the road.

Miscellaneous

Drugs: Bring any prescription drugs you may need.

Band-aids, pain killers, and any personal prescriptions are included in the first-aid kit.

Use a travel guidebook or maps to help you explore the region.

Snacks: Bring some energy bars or snacks with you for long days out.

Check the weather prediction for your vacation dates so you can adapt your packing appropriately. Pack light and allow

space for any keepsakes you may wish to bring back. Have a
wonderful time in Costa Brava!

Chapter Three

Top Attractions & Historical Monuments in Costa Brava

The Costa Brava is well-known for its stunning coastline scenery, picturesque communities, and rich cultural legacy. There are several historical monuments along the Costa Brava that represent the region's history and architectural traditions. The following are some noteworthy cultural and historical monuments in the Costa Brava:

Tossa de Mar Castle: This ancient castle, located in the town of Tossa de Mar, goes back to the 12th century. It was constructed to protect the town from pirate raids. The castle has a historical museum and gives spectacular views of the shoreline.

Sant Pere de Rodes Monastery: This Benedictine monastery, located near the town of Port de la Selva, goes back to the 10th century. It is a fine example of Romanesque construction, with an outstanding bell tower and a lovely cloister.

Palamós Fishing Museum: Palamós is a fishing village on the Costa Brava, and its fishing museum provides information on the region's marine history. Traditional fishing boats, gear, and displays about the local fishing business are on display at the museum.

Peralada Castle: This 14th-century medieval castle is located in the municipality of Peralada. It has a long history and is currently home to a cultural foundation that includes a library, wine museum, and casino.

Sant Feliu de Guxols Monastery: Founded in the 10th century, this Benedictine monastery is situated in Sant Feliu de Guixols. It has a lovely church with an amazing bell tower and hosts a number of cultural events throughout the year.

These are only a few examples of cultural and historical sites around the Costa Brava. The area has a wide diversity of architectural styles and historical buildings that highlight its rich cultural history.

Costa Brava Top Attractions

Costa Brava is a lovely coastal area in northern Catalonia, Spain, famed for its beautiful beaches, attractive communities, and rich cultural legacy. Here are some of the most popular tourist sites in Costa Brava:

Besal: A lovely medieval town with a charming bridge, cobblestone lanes, and an intriguing Jewish section. One of the features of Besal is the beautiful 11th-century Romanesque bridge.

Figueres: Salvador Dal's birthplace and home to the Dali Theatre-Museum. This bizarre museum displays a large collection of the artist's works, providing a unique insight into his creative mind.

Girona is a lively city with a long history. Explore the medieval old town, stroll along the historic city walls, see the towering Girona Cathedral, and see the colorful buildings along the Onyar River.

Lloret de Mar is a renowned tourist resort known for its bustling nightlife and stunning beaches. Aside from the beaches, there are also the lovely Santa Clotilde Gardens and the old Sant Joan Castle.

Blanes is a beautiful seaside town known for its floral gardens, Marimurtra and Pinya de Rosa. These gardens have a wide assortment of plant species from all over the globe, as well as breathtaking views of the shoreline.

The Medes Islands are a series of tiny islands near L'Estartit. Because of its abundant marine life and crystal-clear seas, it is a popular diving and snorkeling destination.

These are just a handful of the numerous attractions on offer in Costa Brava. This location has plenty to offer any sort of tourist, whether they are interested in history, wildlife, or just resting on gorgeous beaches.

Contemporary Art Galleries And Museums

There are some famous modern art galleries and museums in the Costa Brava area that are worth seeing. While the Costa Brava is more known for its beautiful coastal views and charming villages, there are a few spots where you can see modern art. Here are several possibilities:

Espai Carmen Thyssen - Sant Feliu de Guixols: This art space in Sant Feliu de Guixols hosts contemporary art exhibits exhibiting works by both local and international artists. It is a division of the Carmen Thyssen Museum in Barcelona, and it features a wide variety of creative styles and materials.

Torroella de Montgrí Museum of the Mediterranean: This museum focuses on Mediterranean culture and art, including modern pieces. It presents rotating exhibits that often include modern artists and explore a variety of subjects relating to the region's past and current challenges.

Vila Casas Foundation - Palamós: The Vila Casas Foundation in Palamós has a collection of modern Catalan art, however it is not entirely focused on it. The foundation has many locations around Catalonia, one of which being Espai Carmen Thyssen in Palamós.

MAC - Museum of Contemporary Art - Figueres: The Dali Theatre-Museum is located in Figueres, which is recognized as the birthplace of surrealist artist Salvador Dal. However, the museum also has a section devoted to modern art, which displays works by diverse artists.

La Sala - Palafrugell: La Sala is a Palafrugell art center that promotes contemporary art exhibits and cultural activities. It showcases temporary exhibits of works by emerging and renowned artists, and it serves as a venue for modern creative expression.

Please keep in mind that the Costa Brava region's contemporary art scene may not be as broad as that of big cities like Barcelona. Check the schedules and exhibits of these places ahead of time to ensure they correspond with your interests.

National Parks And Reserve

The Costa Brava is a lovely coastal area in northeastern Spain, notably in the Catalan province of Girona. While it lacks a designated national park, it is home to various natural parks and reserves with beautiful scenery and wildlife. Here are a few examples:

Cap de Creus Natural Park: This park, located on the Iberian Peninsula's easternmost point, is famed for its rough coastal cliffs, rocky landscapes, and crystal-clear seas. It is Catalonia's biggest maritime-terrestrial natural park.

Aiguamolls de l'Empordà Natural Park: This wetland reserve in the Empordà plain is a refuge for birdwatchers and environment aficionados. It is home to a variety of bird species such as flamingos, herons, and ducks.

Natural Park of Montgr, Medes Islands, and Baix Ter: This park contains many natural ecosystems, including the Montgr mountain range, the Medes Islands archipelago (a famous diving destination), and the Baix Ter marshes.

Cad-Moixeró Natural Park: Located in the Pyrenees Mountains, this park is not exactly on the Costa Brava. It has beautiful mountain scenery, hiking routes, and winter sports activities.

Cap de Creus Maritime-Terrestrial National Park: This protected region, which is next to the Cap de Creus Natural Park, includes both land and water. It protects the area's unique maritime environment and wildlife.

Hiking, birding, snorkeling, and just enjoying the natural beauty of the Costa Brava area are all possible in these parks and reserves.

Gardens and Romantic Couples Packs

Costa Brava is a lovely beach location noted for its romantic vibe. Here are a few choices for romantic couples packs and gardens in Costa Brava:

Cap Roig Botanical Garden: Located near the village of Palafrugell, Cap Roig Botanical Garden is a wonderful area to spend time with your sweetheart. It has spectacular views of the Mediterranean Sea and a diverse collection of plant species from all over the globe. The park also organizes a variety of cultural activities, such as music performances, making it a great location for a romantic evening.

Marimurtra Botanical Garden: Marimurtra Botanical Garden, located in Blanes, is yet another wonderful Costa Brava excursion. It has approximately 4,000 plant kinds and provides breathtaking views of the shoreline. Couples will undoubtedly appreciate strolling hand in hand amid the garden's rich foliage and colorful blossoms.

Santa Clotilde Gardens: Santa Clotilde Gardens, located in Lloret de Mar, is a hidden treasure nestled away on a rock overlooking the sea. Its exquisite architecture, which incorporates neoclassical and Renaissance elements, produces a tranquil and romantic atmosphere. Take a leisurely stroll around the garden's terraces, sculptures, and fountains, and bask in the peace.

Jardins de Cap Roig: Located near Calella de Palafrugell, these gardens provide a lovely combination of natural beauty and art. The tiered garden, which is filled with statues and well groomed flora, provides breathtaking views of the Mediterranean. Couples may have a picnic or a peaceful time on one of the garden's chairs while immersed in the romantic ambience.

Pinya de Rosa Tropical Botanical Garden: Located in Blanes, Pinya de Rosa Tropical Botanical Garden is a one-of-a-kind Costa Brava attraction. This garden, known for its extensive collection of tropical and subtropical plants, produces a beautiful and exotic atmosphere. While enjoying the presence of your loved one, explore the bright blossoms and inhale the aromatic smells.

When arranging a visit to these gardens, verify their opening hours and any special criteria or limitations that may be in place, since they may differ. Costa Brava's romantic couples packs and gardens are the ideal setting for making amazing moments with your sweetheart in a lovely and tranquil setting.

Festivals & Events In Costa Brava

The area conducts a variety of festivals and events throughout the year to highlight its rich history, customs, and cultural legacy. Here are some of the major festivals and events that take place in Costa Brava:

Temps de Flors (Girona Flower Festival): This yearly event in May turns Girona into a flowery paradise. Extensive floral displays cover streets, patios, and monuments, creating a beautiful and pleasant ambience.

Festival de la Porta Ferrada: Located in the town of Sant Feliu de Guixols, this famous summer festival presents a wide program of music, dance, theater, and visual arts. It draws both national and international artists and takes place over many weeks from July to August.

Cap Roig Festival: This music festival, held in the gorgeous botanical gardens of Cap Roig in the town of Calella de Palafrugell, brings together top national and international musicians in a spectacular outdoor environment. The event is normally held from July through August.

Festa Major de Roses: In August, the town of Roses celebrates its annual Festa Major, which includes a variety of activities such as traditional dances, parades, concerts, fireworks, and athletic events. It is a colorful event that draws both residents and tourists.

Lloret de Mar's Festa Major takes place in late July or early August, and is a famous tourist attraction. Street parties, music concerts, traditional dances, firework displays, and a parade of giants are all part of the celebration.

Cadaqués International Music Festival: This globally famous music festival is held in the gorgeous seaside town of Cadaqués. It features classical music performances by world-renowned performers and orchestras. The event is typically held in July and August.

Girona's celebration (Fires de Sant Narcs): In late October, Girona commemorates its patron saint, Sant Narcs, with a week-long celebration. Concerts, exhibits, street performances, processions, and different cultural and athletic events bring the city to life.

The Carnival of Palafrugell, held in February, is a spectacular event that includes parades, costumes, music, and dancing. It is a joyous occasion that draws both residents and visitors.

These are only a handful of the festivals and events that occur in the Costa Brava area. Before arranging your vacation, please double-check the particular dates and specifics of each event, since certain events may change from year to year.

Chapter Four

Costa Brava Eco Friendly Accommodations and Their Price Rates

Costa Brava, in northeastern Spain, has a wealth of lodgings that give travelers relaxation, comfort, and a broad range of social services. Whether you're looking for a tranquil spa getaway or a bustling seaside resort, Costa Brava offers something for everyone.

There are many beautiful spa resorts in the area where tourists may engage in revitalizing treatments and therapies. These spas provide a calm and tranquil ambience, making them an ideal respite from the rigors of everyday life. Guests may enjoy a selection of massages, facials, and body treatments suited to their specific requirements, thanks to expert therapists and cutting-edge equipment.

Comfort is a key concern in Costa Brava lodgings, and the hotels and resorts in the region go to great lengths to ensure that their customers have a nice stay. The rooms are attractively constructed, with contemporary facilities and comfortable furniture. There are alternatives to suit all budgets and interests, ranging from big apartments with panoramic views to private villas with exclusive access to pools and gardens. Costa Brava lodgings provide a variety of social facilities to improve the overall visitor experience. Many resorts provide a variety of eating alternatives, from fine dining restaurants to informal cafés, where tourists may sample local and foreign food. Furthermore, pubs and lounges offer a pleasant setting in which to enjoy a refreshing beverage or socialize with other tourists.

Tourists may use the many amenities offered for leisure and enjoyment, such as swimming pools, fitness centers, tennis courts, and golf courses. Some motels also offer leisure activities and trips for visitors to discover the region's spectacular natural beauty.

Finally, Costa Brava lodgings provide a well-balanced mix of leisure, comfort, and social facilities. In this lovely Spanish area, you may discover the right location to relax and have a wonderful holiday, whether you prefer tranquility in a spa retreat or excitement in a seaside resort.

Budget-Friendly Tourist Hotels & Resorts

The Costa Brava is a stunning coastal area in northern Spain famed for its rocky cliffs, gorgeous beaches, and quaint seaside villages. While there are various budget-friendly hotels and resorts in the region, costs might vary based on location, time of year, and particular features provided. Here are a few alternatives for reasonably priced accommodations:

Hotel Aiguablava: This hotel in Begur provides pleasant accommodations with breathtaking views of the Mediterranean Sea. Depending on the season, prices might vary from €70 to €120 each night.

Hotel Montjoi: Located in L'Escala, this hotel offers modest but charming rooms and is a short walk from the beach. Rates normally range between €60 and €90 per night.

Hotel Port-Bo: Located in the picturesque town of Calella de Palafrugell, this hotel is a short walk from gorgeous beaches and provides cheap accommodations in a delightful setting. Prices per night might vary from €60 to €100.

Hotel Garbi: This budget-friendly hotel in Lloret de Mar provides pleasant accommodations and is near to the town center and beach. Prices typically range from €50 to €80 per night.

Camping Cala Llevadó: This camping choice in Tossa de Mar provides a variety of lodging options, including tents, bungalows, and cabins. Camping may be a cost-effective choice depending on the kind of accommodation and season.

Please keep in mind that the prices shown are estimates and may change depending on variables such as availability, seasonal demand, and any special deals or promotions.

Luxury Tourist Hotels & Resorts

Here is a broad overview of various luxury hotels and resorts in the Costa Brava region, along with an estimate of their prices. Please keep in mind that pricing might change based on the time of year, accommodation type, and availability.

Hotel Camiral at PGA Catalunya Resort: Located in Girona, this 5-star hotel provides magnificent rooms, a spa, golf courses, and a variety of services. Room costs normally range between €200 and €300 per night.

Hotel Mas de Torrent: This 5-star hotel in the lovely town of Torrent has magnificent rooms, a spa, an outdoor pool, and gorgeous grounds. Prices per night might vary between €300 and €500.

Hostal de la Gavina: This historic 5-star hotel in the coastal town of S'Agaró provides a magnificent experience with its beachfront setting, outdoor pool, spa, and gourmet dining choices. Room costs typically range from €350 and €600 per night.

Hotel Vistabella: Located in Roses, this 5-star hotel has stunning views of the Mediterranean Sea, a private beach, spa facilities, and a famous restaurant. Prices per night might vary between €300 and €500.

Alva Park Costa Brava: This luxury 5-star hotel in Lloret de Mar has a spa, indoor and outdoor pools, and individual service. Room costs normally range between €400 and €700 per night.

Vacation Rentals and Apartments

In Costa Brava, there are several apartments and holiday rentals to suit a variety of budgets and interests. While I can provide you some broad information, please keep in mind that precise pricing may vary based on location, size, facilities, and the time of year you want to visit.

Apartments and holiday rentals for all budgets may be found in famous tourist destinations such as Lloret de Mar, Tossa de Mar, and Blanes. Prices often vary according to the amount of bedrooms, closeness to the beach, and overall property quality.

Prices tend to be higher during the peak summer season, which normally runs from June through August, compared to other periods of the year. Rates may be more inexpensive during the shoulder seasons of spring and fall.

A typical one-bedroom apartment in Costa Brava may be expected to cost between €50 and €100 per night. Larger flats or luxury rentals might cost between €100 and €300 per night or more.

It's worth mentioning that, particularly during peak season, certain apartments and holiday rentals may need a minimum stay of a few nights or a week. Furthermore, some hotels may demand extra costs for cleaning, security deposits, or other services.

I suggest reviewing major accommodation booking websites or calling local rental agencies to receive the most current and up-to-date information on individual apartments or vacation rentals in Costa Brava. Based on your precise vacation dates and interests, they will give you full information on availability, facilities, and rates.

Tourists Hostels and Guesthouses

Costa Brava is a renowned tourist destination in northeastern Spain noted for its magnificent beaches, picturesque coastal villages, and rich cultural history. Guesthouses and hostels are fantastic places to stay if you're seeking cheap lodging in Costa Brava. Here is some information on Costa Brava guesthouses and hostels, as well as their estimated costs:

Guesthouses:

Guesthouses on the Costa Brava are typically tiny enterprises that provide individual rooms with communal or en-suite bathrooms. In comparison to bigger hotels, they provide a more customized and private experience. Guesthouse prices might vary based on location, facilities, and season.

In low season (off-peak), guesthouses may be found for roughly €30 to €60 per night for a twin room.

Prices for a double room in high season (peak tourist season) may vary from €50 to €100 or more per night.

It is crucial to remember that these rates are estimates and may vary depending on criteria such as location, lodging quality, and included facilities.

Hostels:

Hostels are low-cost lodging choices that often include dormitory-style rooms with shared amenities such as restrooms and common spaces. Backpackers, lone travelers, and those wishing to meet other travelers flock to them.

Hostel costs in Costa Brava range from around €15 to €30 per night for a stay in a dormitory room.

Private rooms at hostels are also available at a higher price, ranging from around €40 to €80 per night for a double room, depending on location and amenities.

Again, these are estimates that may vary depending on variables such as location, facilities, and season.

It's worth noting that prices in famous tourist locations like Girona, Tossa de Mar, and Lloret de Mar may be costlier, whilst smaller towns or less touristic places may offer more cheap choices. Furthermore, costs might change during special events, festivals, or holidays, so it's best to book ahead of time and confirm pricing with the individual guesthouse or hostel.

When looking for a place to stay, use online travel platforms like Booking.com, Hostelworld, or Airbnb to compare costs, read reviews, and pick the best alternative for your preferences and budget.

Costa Brava Tourist Camp Venues

Tourists may camp in a number of locations in the Costa Brava area of northeastern Spain. Here are a few common solutions, along with an estimate of their costs:

Camping Internacional de Calonge: This campground is situated in Calonge, near the Costa Brava's lovely beaches. It has large tent pitches as well as rental facilities such as bungalows and mobile homes. The cost per night fluctuates between €20 and €40, depending on the season and kind of lodging.

Camping Mas Nou: Camping Mas Nou, located in the town of Castelló d'Empuries, is a family-friendly campsite with outstanding amenities such as swimming pools, sports courts, and entertainment programs. A pitch costs roughly €30 to €40 per night, while rented lodgings cost between €50 and €100.

Camping Tucan: Camping Tucan, located in Lloret de Mar, is a popular option for travelers wishing to experience the area's busy nightlife and beaches. The campground has tent spaces as well as mobile homes and bungalows. The average nightly rate is between €30 and €50, depending on the season and kind of lodging.

Camping Cala Llevadó is located in Tossa de Mar and is recognized for its spectacular coastal location and easy access to isolated beaches. It provides tent pitches as well as numerous sorts of rental lodgings. The cost per night for plots is from €30 to €50 and from €60 to €120 for rental lodgings.

Please keep in mind that these are estimates and that actual prices may vary based on the season, the size of the camping group, and the unique facilities and services offered by each campground. It's always a good idea to check with particular campsites for the most up-to-date pricing and availability information based on the time of year you're going.

Chapter Five

Costa Brava Nightlife At A Glance

Costa Brava, in northern Spain, is renowned for its beautiful coastline and lively nightlife. Visitors visiting Costa Brava are in for a treat when it comes to nightlife. The area provides a broad and thrilling experience for partygoers, with a profusion of pubs, clubs, and entertainment alternatives.

Costa Brava has a diverse nightlife scene that caters to a variety of interests and inclinations. There's something for everyone, whether you want fashionable beach clubs, exciting music places, or comfortable pubs. The location is especially well-known for its beach parties, where you can dance the night away with your toes in the sand beneath a starry sky. The bright and dynamic environment is one of the attractions of Costa Brava's nightlife scene. Locals and visitors alike are recognized for their joy and enjoyment of having a good time. Costa Brava nightlife is generally defined by bright music, enthusiastic dancing, and a feeling of freedom and pleasure.

In addition to entertainment, Costa Brava nightlife provides a chance to flex and flaunt your style. Many clubs and pubs have dress rules, which encourage attendees to dress up and flaunt their fashion sense. It's a chance to see and be seen, with individuals dressed to impress and relishing the spotlight.

Overall, Costa Brava nightlife is a thrilling experience packed with music, dancing, and a dynamic environment. Whether you want to party till morning or just enjoy a few drinks in a vibrant atmosphere, Costa Brava has a variety of alternatives to guarantee a wonderful night out.

A Guide to Costa Brava City Bars and Nightclubs

If you want to visit the city pubs and nightclubs in Costa Brava, here is a guide to help you make the most of your visit:

Lloret de Mar is a Town in Spain.

Tropics: Tropics, located in the center of Lloret de Mar, is one of the area's most popular nightclubs. It has many dance floors, live DJs, and a fun environment.

Revolution: This club features a variety of music genres such as R&B, hip-hop, and house. It boasts a large dance floor and a lively party vibe.

Londoner: Londoner, a British-style pub with a bustling ambiance, is a terrific spot to start your night with drinks and live sports before hitting the clubs.

Torre del Mar:

Bahia Beach Club: Located on the oceanfront, Bahia Beach Club has a laid-back and stylish vibe. It's a fantastic spot for drinks, live music, and stunning views of the Mediterranean Sea.

Magma: A renowned nightclub in Tossa de Mar, Magma is known for its dynamic environment. It has live DJs spinning a range of music genres and a combination of indoor and outdoor areas.

El Barco: Located in Tossa de Mar's historic district, El Barco is a charming tavern that often holds live music performances. It's a nice place to chill with a couple beers.

Blanes:

Disco Tropics: One of Blanes' largest and most well-known nightclubs, Disco Tropics has many dance floors, live entertainment, and a bustling party atmosphere. It is well-known for its high-energy concerts and excellent music.

Pacha Blanes: Pacha Blanes, a well-known branch of the world recognized Pacha nightclub brand, provides a sophisticated setting, superb music, and a sumptuous environment.

Barca d'Or: Located near the marina, Barca d'Or is a sophisticated pub with a diverse menu of cocktails and beverages. It's a terrific spot to start your evening before venturing out into Blanes' nightlife.

Roses:

Moli de Roses: Moli de Roses is a beach club and lounge bar located in a gorgeous setting overlooking the sea. It has a laid-back vibe, comfy seating, and wonderful beverages.

Bon Viatge Music bar: This Roses bar is noted for its live music performances, which include a variety of genres like rock, blues, and jazz. It's a comfortable area to drink while listening to fantastic music.

Sky Bar by Aqua Hotel: Located on the Aqua Hotel's rooftop, Sky Bar provides panoramic views of Roses. It's a hip and fashionable area to drink cocktails and watch the sunset.

Check the opening hours and dress rules of the places you want to visit, since they may differ. Additionally, having a designated driver or using public transit is always a smart option to guarantee a safe night out.

How to Locate Live Music Venues and Jazz Clubs

Follow these procedures to locate live music venues and jazz bars in Costa Brava:

Online Search: Begin by performing an internet search using search engines or local directories. To narrow down your searches, use keywords like "live music venues Costa Brava" or "jazz bars Costa Brava." This will provide you a list of clubs and pubs that are recognized for presenting live music events.

Local Event Listings: Look for websites, online forums, or community boards that list forthcoming events in Costa Brava. These platforms often include live music events, including jazz concerts. Examine the event descriptions for individual venues or pubs.

Social Media: Explore social media networks like Facebook, Instagram, and Twitter. Many Costa Brava establishments and pubs have social media profiles where they advertise forthcoming events and post information about live music performances. To find postings about live music in the region, look for appropriate hashtags such as #CostaBravaMusic or #JazzBarsCostaBrava.

Local Guides and publications: Look for Costa Brava entertainment and nightlife guides and publications. These periodicals often provide suggestions and evaluations of jazz clubs and live music venues. Check out their websites or get actual copies from local businesses or tourist information centers.

Ask Locals or Hotel personnel: When you arrive in Costa Brava, get suggestions from locals or hotel personnel. They are likely to be acquainted with the area's prominent live music venues and jazz pubs and may give you useful information or hidden treasures.

TripAdvisor or Yelp: Make use of popular review sites such as TripAdvisor or Yelp. Listings and user evaluations for different places, such as live music venues and jazz bars, are often included on these sites. To help you make educated selections, you may refine the search results by location and read feedback from past guests.

Before attending any venue or jazz bar, check the calendar and confirm the availability of live music performances, since events might change by day and hour.

Live Music and Jazz Venues

Costa Brava has a thriving music culture, with several live music and jazz establishments.

Here are a few popular venues in Costa Brava that have previously held live music and jazz concerts. Festival de Jazz de Girona: This yearly jazz festival is held in Girona, near the Costa Brava. The festival brings together world-renowned jazz artists and showcases concerts in a variety of locations across the city.

Sunset Jazz Club, Lloret de Mar: The Sunset Jazz Club, located in the seaside village of Lloret de Mar, provides a quiet and private atmosphere for jazz fans. The facility often presents live jazz concerts by local and international performers.

El Celler de la Música, Figueres: Located near the Costa Brava, El Celler de la Musica is a famous venue for live music performances such as jazz. It offers a lively environment and showcases a range of concerts of all genres.

Jazzman Jazz Club, Blanes: Another venue noted for live jazz concerts is Jazzman Jazz Club in Blanes. It often features great local jazz performers and sometimes invites guest artists.

Jazz & Blues Café, Roses: Jazz & Blues Café, located in Roses, provides a relaxed ambiance and showcases live jazz and blues performances. It's a nice place to listen to music while sipping a drink or eating a meal.

Remember that the availability of live music and jazz events might vary, particularly during the off-season. To receive the most up-to-date information on performances and schedules, check with local tourist offices, event listings, or the websites/social media pages of these venues.

Tips for a Memorable Nightlife in Costa Brava

If you want to enjoy a wonderful night in Costa Brava, consider the following suggestions:

- Explore the seaside villages: Tossa de Mar, Cadaqués, and Lloret de Mar are just a few of the wonderful coastal towns on the Costa Brava. Take an evening walk down the shoreline to take in the scenery and soak up the ambiance.

- Enjoy the local food: Costa Brava is famous for its exquisite Mediterranean cuisine. Enjoy a spectacular supper at a beachfront restaurant, where you can sample fresh seafood dishes, tapas, and regional favorites like paella or fideuà. Don't forget to drink some local wine or sangria with your dinner.

- Enjoy the nightlife: The Costa Brava has a thriving nightlife culture, especially in prominent towns such as Lloret de Mar and Blanes. Discover the vibrant pubs, clubs, and discos that come to life after dark. Dance to worldwide and local music, see live acts, and socialize with both residents and visitors.

- Attend a cultural event: Check the local event calendar to see if any concerts, festivals, or cultural events are scheduled during your stay. Throughout the year, Costa Brava offers a variety of events including music festivals, traditional holidays, and art exhibits. Attending one of these events may give your night a one-of-a-kind and unforgettable twist.

- Sunset views: Look for the finest sites along the shore to watch beautiful sunset views. Watching the sun set over the Mediterranean Sea from a hilltop, a seaside tavern, or a rocky cliff may be an unforgettable experience.

- Take a moonlit beach walk: After the sun has gone down, go along the beach in the moonlight. The Costa Brava coastline has several beautiful beaches where you may enjoy the peace and quiet of the night, listen to the waves, and feel the sand under your feet.

- Participate in water activities: If you like adventure, try engaging in water activities such as night kayaking or paddleboarding. Some firms provide guided cruises that take you beneath the stars to explore the beaches and aquatic life. It's a one-of-a-kind approach to make your Costa Brava night absolutely memorable.

- Relax at a beachside lounge: For a more laid-back evening, seek out a beachfront lounge or bar where you can unwind in comfy seats while sipping a glass or two. Many establishments provide chill-out music, warm atmospheres, and breathtaking sea views, enabling you to relax and make unforgettable memories.

Remember to respect the local culture and appreciate the beauty of Costa Brava as you construct your own unforgettable night.

Chapter Six

Costa Brava Food and Drinks

Costa Brava is well-known for its delicious meals and refreshing beverages. Costa Brava food represents a complex combination of Mediterranean and Catalan tastes, producing a one-of-a-kind and spectacular gastronomic experience. Seafood takes center stage in Costa Brava cuisine, with fresh catches of the day converted into delectable meals. Suquet, a typical seafood stew, is served with succulent prawns, octopus, and sardines. The olive oil from the surrounding Empordà area gives a distinctive and delectable flavor to every meal.

Costa Brava is particularly well-known for traditional Catalan foods like pa amb tomàquet (bread rubbed with ripe tomatoes and drizzled with olive oil), fideuà (a paella-like dish prepared with short noodles), and i carn d'olla (a substantial meat and vegetable stew). These meals exemplify the region's culinary tradition.

Costa Brava provides a variety of delectable beverages to accompany the wonderful food. Local wines, such as sparkling cava, crisp white wines, and strong reds from the Empordà area, complement meals nicely. Also popular for a quiet day or evening are the cool sangria and local vermouth.

To summarize, Costa Brava's food and beverages take the taste buds on a delightful trip, mixing the freshness of the Mediterranean with the rich flavors of Catalan cuisine. It's a real treat for foodies looking for a genuine and outstanding gastronomic experience.

Favorite Food & Cuisine

The Costa Brava has a delicious variety of food and cuisines that will gratify any gourmet connoisseur. Here are some of the most popular meals and cuisines in Costa Brava:

Paella: A must-try in Costa Brava is this renowned Spanish meal. It's a savory rice meal that may be made with fish, chicken, rabbit, or veggies.

Carn d'olla Escudella: This substantial Catalan stew is a popular meal throughout the winter months. It is often composed of meats such as hog, beef, and veal, as well as vegetables and legumes.

Suquet de Peix: Because the Costa Brava is a coastline location, seafood dishes abound. Suquet de Peix is a classic fish stew that includes fresh fish, shellfish, potatoes, garlic, and tomatoes. It's flavorful and a genuine joy for seafood fans.

Botifarra: This Catalan sausage is composed of pork and seasoned with garlic, pepper, and nutmeg. It's great grilled, pan-fried, or in stews and casseroles.

Crema Catalana: Crema Catalana is a popular dessert in Catalonia that is comparable to crème brûlée. It is covered with a coating of caramelized sugar and has a creamy custard foundation flavored with lemon or orange zest.

Red & White wine: Costa Brava is well-known for its exceptional wine production, notably in the Empordà area. The wines made here are both red and white, with distinct qualities inspired by the Mediterranean environment.

Catalan Cava: Catalonia is well-known for its sparkling wine, Cava. Cava, in the traditional way, is a delectable alternative to enjoy as an aperitif or to complement your meals.

L'Escala anchovies: L'Escala, a town in Costa Brava, is well-known for its high-quality anchovies. These little, delicious fish are typically salt-cured and may be eaten alone or in a variety of recipes.

These are just a handful of the delectable meals and cuisines available in Costa Brava. The area is rich in culinary traditions and provides a diverse array of possibilities for food enthusiasts to discover and enjoy.

Vegan and Vegetarian Options

The Costa Brava has a range of vegetarian and vegan food alternatives. While traditional Catalan cuisine is recognized for its emphasis on fish and meat, many local restaurants have evolved to meet the rising demand for plant-based meals. Here are some possibilities to consider:

Vegetarian and Vegan Restaurants: The Costa Brava area has a number of vegetarian and vegan restaurants that specialize on plant-based food. These restaurants provide a variety of meals such as burgers, salads, wraps, pasta, and more. L'Aixada Vegetariana in Girona and La Vida Fàcil in Lloret de Mar are two famous vegetarian restaurants.

Local Catalan Cuisine: While traditional Catalan cuisine is heavy on meat and fish, vegetarian and vegan choices are available. Look for (roasted vegetables), pa amb tomàquet (tomato bread), (ratatouille), and pan con chocolate (chocolate spread).

Tapas and Pintxos Bars: Vegetarian and vegan choices are available at many tapas and pintxos bars in the Costa Brava area. Patatas bravas (fried potatoes with spicy tomato sauce), padron peppers, grilled veggies, tortilla de patatas (potato omelet), and numerous bread-based tapas are available. Simply ask the staff for vegetarian or vegan alternatives, and they will point you in the right direction.

Mediterranean Cuisine: Because of its closeness to the Mediterranean Sea, the Costa Brava area has an abundance of fresh fruits, vegetables, and Mediterranean ingredients. Gazpacho (chilled tomato soup), Mediterranean salads, grilled vegetables with olive oil, and vegetable paella are also good choices.

International Cuisine: There are many international restaurants on the Costa Brava that cater to vegetarian and vegan inclinations. You may find vegetarian and vegan food on the menus of Indian, Italian, Mexican, and Middle Eastern eateries.

It's usually a good idea to let the restaurant staff know about any dietary preferences or limitations so that they can appropriately fulfill your demands. Online restaurant directories and review sites may also give more particular information on vegetarian and vegan-friendly restaurants in the Costa Brava area.

Best Cafes & Restaurants

The Costa Brava area of northern Spain is famous for its breathtaking coastline, lovely beaches, and delectable gastronomy. Here are some of the greatest Costa Brava cafés and restaurants:

El Celler de Can Roca (Girona): This world-famous restaurant has three Michelin stars and has been rated one of the top restaurants in the world on several occasions. It serves unique and imaginative Catalan cuisine made using locally obtained ingredients.

Les Cols (Olot): Les Cols is another Michelin-starred restaurant recognized for its simple décor and outstanding food. The restaurant serves contemporary Catalan cuisine made with fresh, seasonal, and locally produced ingredients.

Compartir (Cadaqués): With its idea of sharing plates, Compartir provides a unique eating experience in the gorgeous seaside town of Cadaqués. Tapas-style meals with a unique twist are served at the restaurant.

Can Pujol (Tamariu): Can Pujol is a renowned seafood restaurant located in the picturesque town of Tamariu. It is well-known for its fresh fish and seafood dishes made with Catalan tastes.

La Gamba (Llafranc): The seafood restaurant La Gamba is located in the seaside town of Llafranc. It is well-known for its fresh seafood, particularly its prawns, which are a local delicacy. The restaurant has stunning views of the Mediterranean Sea.

Sa Rascassa (Pals): A hidden treasure famed for its magnificent beach setting and delicious seafood, Sa Rascassa is located near the historic town of Pals. The restaurant has a patio that overlooks the sea, providing the ideal setting for dining.

Els Tinars (Llagostera): Els Tinars is a Michelin-starred restaurant serving classic Catalan cuisine with a contemporary twist. It provides a refined dining experience in a pleasant rural environment.

Can Boix (Tossa de Mar): Can Boix is a family-run restaurant recognized for its traditional Mediterranean food. It is located in the scenic village of Tossa de Mar. It provides a wide range of foods, including fresh fish, shellfish, and traditional Catalan fare.

Bar L'Hostal (Begur): Bar L'Hostal is a well-known café and bar in Begur. It has a laid-back environment and serves wonderful tapas, sandwiches, and a range of beverages. It's a terrific place for a quick nibble or a leisurely lunch.

Pastisseria Bubó (Girona): Pastisseria Bubó in Girona is a must-see for anyone with a sweet taste. This famous pastry store provides a large assortment of aesthetically gorgeous and delectable pastries, cakes, and chocolates.

These are just a handful of the many excellent cafés and restaurants in the Costa Brava area. Whether you're seeking for exquisite dining experiences or local culinary pleasures, the Costa Brava has something for everyone.

Etiquette for Dining in Costa Brava

There are a few norms and practices to bear in mind when it comes to eating etiquette in Costa Brava. Here are some pointers to assist you manage Costa Brava eating etiquette:

- Meal Times: When compared to other nations, Spaniards eat their meals later. Lunch is often served between 1:30 and 3:30 pm, while supper is typically served between 9 and 11 pm. Remember this while making restaurant reservations or planning your meals.

- Greetings: When entering a restaurant or other social event, it is usual to greet those already there with a cordial "Hola!" (Hello!) or "Buenas tardes/noches." This demonstrates civility and establishes a pleasant tone.

- Table Manners: It is polite in formal dining occasions to wait for the host or the eldest person at the table to begin eating before you begin. Maintain your hands on the table while resting your wrists on the edge. Elbows are not permitted on the table.

- Bread with Olive Oil: Bread is usually served with meals in Costa Brava. Tear off a slice of bread and hold it in your hand while spreading olive oil with a knife or dipping it in an olive oil dish supplied. Unless expressly requested, do not butter your bread.

- Tapas Culture: Tapas are tiny dishes of cuisine that are shared among diners in Costa Brava. It is customary to order numerous tapas plates to share with your friends while ordering tapas. Remember to take your time and savor the range of tastes.

- Wine and Toasted Cheese: Costa Brava is situated in Catalonia, which is well-known for its wines. It is usual to take a glass of wine when given one. Before taking a drink, establish eye contact with the person you're toasting and say "Salud!" (Cheers!).

- Paying the tab: In Costa Brava, the individual who offers the invitation normally pays the tab. If you are the one who invites, you are required to reimburse the costs. However, it is customary for friends to split dinner costs, so don't be startled if someone insists on paying for you.

- Tipping is not as prevalent in Spain as it is in some other nations. However, giving a little gratuity for excellent service is welcomed. Round up the amount or give a gratuity of 5-10% of the total.

Remember that, although these tips might help you manage Costa Brava dining etiquette, the most essential thing is to relax, enjoy your meal, and appreciate the local traditions and cuisine.

Chapter Seven

What You Should Know Before Visiting Costa Brava

Before traveling to Costa Brava, arm yourself with crucial information and insights, since education is the key to unlocking the full splendors of this coastal paradise.

Costa Brava Money

The Costa Brava is a coastal area in northeastern Spain, in the Catalan province of Girona. Costa Brava is a part of Spain, hence the official currency is the Euro (€). The Euro is the currency of most European Union nations, and it is widely recognized across Spain, including the Costa Brava.

If you intend on visiting Costa Brava, you will require Euros for your transactions. It is recommended that you convert your money into Euros before your trip, either at your local bank or via a currency exchange agency. You may also withdraw Euros from ATMs on the Costa Brava using your debit or credit card, but keep in mind that there may be transaction fees and foreign currency costs connected with using ATMs overseas.

Money Exchange Spots In Costa Brava

You may exchange money at many sites in the Costa Brava area of Spain. Here are some frequent currency conversion options:

Banks: Banks are a dependable and safe way to exchange money. Currency exchange services are provided by major banks in the Costa Brava area, including Banco Sabadell, CaixaBank, and BBVA. To exchange currencies, go to the bank's branch during normal business hours.

Currency Exchange Offices: Currency exchange offices, often known as bureaux de change, may be found in famous tourist sites. These locations specialize in foreign exchange and provide competitive rates. Look for exchange offices at famous tourist areas along the Costa Brava, such as Lloret de Mar, Tossa de Mar, and Blanes.

Post Offices: In Spain, post offices often provide currency exchange services. Find a post office in the Costa Brava region and ask whether they do money exchange. Keep in mind that post offices may have restricted hours of operation, so call ahead to confirm their hours of operation.

If you haven't exchanged your money before arriving in Costa Brava, currency exchange facilities are available at airports and railway stations. However, keep in mind that exchange rates may not be as attractive as at banks or specialist exchange offices.

ATMs: Automated Teller Machines (ATMs) may be found throughout the Costa Brava area. You may use your debit or credit card to withdraw money from ATMs, and the machine will give you the local currency. Check with your bank to see if there are any foreign transaction fees or withdrawal limitations.

Before converting money, examine exchange rates and fees at several sites to guarantee you receive the best bargain. Also, notify your bank or credit card issuer of your trip intentions to prevent problems with card use in a foreign nation.

LGBTQ + Acceptance

Costa Brava is a northeastern Spanish coastal area famed for its magnificent beaches, charming villages, and lively culture. When it comes to LGBTQ+ acceptance, Spain has made considerable progress in recent years, becoming one of the world's most LGBTQ+-friendly nations.

Spain approved same-sex marriage in 2005, making it one of just a handful nations to do so at the time. Since then, the Spanish government has continued to defend and preserve LGBTQ+ rights. Anti-discrimination legislation is in place to protect LGBTQ+ people from discrimination in employment, housing, and public services.

In terms of LGBTQ+ acceptance, Costa Brava is consistent with the progressive views seen across Spain. Visitors and people from a wide spectrum of backgrounds, including LGBTQ+ persons and cultures, flock to the area. There are LGBTQ+-friendly businesses that cater to the LGBTQ+ community, such as pubs, clubs, and motels.

The annual Barcelona Pride, one of Europe's major Pride celebrations, is hosted nearby. Many individuals from Costa

Brava and the neighboring regions attend the events to show their support for LGBTQ+ rights and inclusion.

It is crucial to highlight that opinions regarding LGBTQ+ people may differ from person to person, and there may still be incidents of discrimination or prejudice. Overall, LGBTQ+ acceptance in Costa Brava is good, and LGBTQ+ visitors and residents should feel comfortable and welcome in the area.

Emergency Contacts

The emergency contact numbers in Costa Brava, Spain are:

112 Emergency Services (General)
This number may be contacted in the event of any emergency, including medical crises, accidents, fires, and crimes.

061 Medical Emergencies
Dial 061 to call the emergency medical services (Servicio de Emergencias Médicas) if you need urgent medical treatment.

091 National Police (Polica Nacional)

Contact the National Police if you want to report a crime, a theft, or any other non-life threatening emergency that requires police assistance.

Policia Local (Local Police)
The phone number for the local police in Costa Brava may vary based on the town or municipality. It is best to ask your hotel or the nearby tourist information center for the local police contact number.

Fire Department (Bomberos): 080
In the event of a fire or other fire-related emergency, call 080 to contact the fire department.

Costa Brava Cultural Etiquette

When visiting Costa Brava, it is essential to be aware of local cultural etiquette in order to show respect and have a great experience. Here are some pointers to remember:

- Greetings: Greetings in Costa Brava are often warm and pleasant. When meeting someone for the first time, it is customary to exchange a handshake as well as a verbal greeting such as "Hola" (hello) or "Buenos das" (good morning). Because Spanish is the official language, knowing a few fundamental phrases is beneficial.

- While Costa Brava is a famous tourist destination, it is nonetheless polite to dress modestly while visiting religious sites or attending formal functions. Beachwear is acceptable for the beach, but while visiting cities or eating at restaurants, dress casually and neatly.

- Punctuality: Time is rather flexible in Spanish culture, and punctuality may not be as stringent as in other cultures. Arriving on time for appointments, meetings, or dinner reservations is still considered courteous. Arriving a few minutes late is normally okay if you've been asked to someone's house.

- Table manners: In comparison to other nations, Spanish mealtimes are often late. Lunch is usually served between 2:00 and 3:00 PM, while supper is usually served between 9:00 and 10:00 PM. It is usual to wait for the host or hostess to advise where you should sit while eating out. It is customary to keep your hands on the table throughout the meal and to exchange food and participate in active discussion.

- Tipping is appreciated but not required in Costa Brava. If you've had excellent service, a 5-10% tip is often regarded as reasonable. Some restaurants, however, may impose a service fee on the bill. If you're doubtful, always double-check the bill or contact the staff.

- While English is often spoken in tourist regions, knowing a few simple Spanish words may go a long way toward demonstrating respect for the local culture. Your attempts to converse in their language would be appreciated by the people.

- Cultural places and traditions: It is crucial to dress modestly and follow any regulations or standards in place while visiting cultural sites such as churches or historical structures. Photography may be limited or forbidden in certain circumstances, so verify before taking images.

By following these cultural etiquette guidelines, you may improve your experience in Costa Brava and create healthy relationships with the people. Have a great time!

Chapter Eight

Traveling on a Budget in Costa Brava

A tourist's financial preparation and management are critical while arranging a visit to Costa Brava. Proper financial preparation ensures that your finances are used properly, enabling you to maximize your vacation without overpaying. It assists you in creating a realistic budget and estimating expenditures for lodging, transportation, food, and activities. You may prioritize activities that are important to you by managing your funds properly, such as visiting famous landmarks or sampling local food. Furthermore, financial preparation helps you to prepare for unforeseen expenditures, emergencies, or other charges that may happen during your vacation. Finally, smart financial preparation and management provide you peace of mind and allow you to have a wonderful and worry-free holiday.

Top Money Saving Strategies

Here are some great money-saving recommendations if you're planning a vacation to Costa Brava and want to save money:

Consider visiting Costa Brava during the shoulder season, which is the time period immediately before or after the high tourist season. Accommodations, airfare, and activities are often cheaper during this period.

1: Plan ahead of time: To get the best offers and discounts, plan your hotels, flights, and activities well in advance. This enables you to take advantage of early bird discounts and receive lower pricing.

2: Stay at cheap lodgings: Instead of high-end hotels, choose budget-friendly options such as guesthouses, hostels, or vacation rentals. These alternatives might be less expensive while still providing decent lodgings.

3: Cook your own meals: Cooking part of your meals at home may help you save money on eating out. Choose motels with kitchens so you may create basic meals using goods from markets and grocery shops in your area. This manner, you may also sample the local food on a tighter budget.

4: Eat like a local: When dining out, choose local eateries and street food vendors over tourist traps. Not only will you get a more real experience, but the pricing will typically be lower.

5: utilizing public transit is often less expensive than renting a vehicle or utilizing cabs. Use buses, trains, and boats to navigate about Costa Brava and see the various locations. This might save you money on transportation expenses.

6: Take advantage of free or low-cost activities: Costa Brava has a plethora of free or low-cost activities. Explore hiking paths, public parks, and picturesque towns while enjoying the magnificent beaches. Investigate local events and festivals that may be taking place during your stay, since they often offer free entertainment.

7: Avoid famous tourist sites: Some of the most popular tourist attractions in Costa Brava may have steep admission costs. Instead, consider visiting off-the-beaten-path places or enjoying the region's natural beauties. You may still have an unforgettable event without spending a fortune.

8: Look for local discounts, coupons, and promotional deals for area attractions, events, and restaurants. Look for any accessible offers at local tourist information centers, websites, or travel guidebooks.

9: Stay hydrated and bring food: Bottled water and snacks might be pricey in tourist regions. Bring a reusable water bottle that you can refill at public drinking fountains. Carry some snacks with you to avoid paying for pricey meals while on the run.

Remember that conserving money does not imply foregoing an enjoyable time. You may have a good experience touring Costa Brava on a budget by preparing ahead, making wise decisions, and being cautious of your expenditures.

Bargaining and Negotiation Strategies

Bargaining and haggling are widespread practices in Costa Brava, particularly at local markets, souvenir stores, and when hiring services. Here are some pointers to assist you efficiently handle the negotiation process:

Conduct your research: Before engaging in any negotiation, it is critical to have a broad sense of the pricing range for the item or service in question. To determine the average cost, do internet research or speak with locals. This information will provide you with a starting point for discussion.

Maintain a polite and courteous demeanor: Bargaining should be seen as an enjoyable and participatory process rather than a combative one. Approach the discussion with a grin on your face, be courteous, and keep a respectful tone throughout. Building a good connection with the seller might be advantageous.

Begin with a low-ball offer: Begin the discussion by proposing a far lower price than you are prepared to pay. This allows the seller to counteroffer, and you may progressively raise your price if necessary. Remember to keep your first offer reasonable and fair.

Use cash: When dealing with small firms or local marketplaces, cash may be a helpful negotiating weapon. When sellers have cash in hand, they may be more willing to haggle since they may avoid credit card fees or other transaction charges.

Bundle things or services: If you want to buy many items or services from the same supplier, consider combining them and negotiating a package pricing. When sellers sense the possibility of a bigger transaction, they may be more ready to offer you a discount.

Be prepared to walk away: Sometimes the greatest negotiation strategy is to be ready to walk away if you can't reach an agreement. This demonstrates to the seller that you are serious, which may cause them to rethink their offer. However, keep in mind that walking away may result in you not receiving the goods or service you want.

Consider the value of the thing or service you're negotiating for, not just the price: While it's crucial to negotiate for a fair price, you should also consider the value of the item or service you're bargaining for. Quality, workmanship, and entire experience should all be considered in your selection, rather than just the lowest price.

Remember that negotiation and negotiating traditions vary across cultures and circumstances. Bargaining is often more tolerated in markets and smaller places in Costa Brava than in bigger retail shops or high-end restaurants.

Top Costa Brava Budget Markets

Costa Brava is a renowned tourist destination in northeastern Spain noted for its magnificent coastline, picturesque villages, and cultural attractions. While there are many markets in the area, these are some of the best budget markets in Costa Brava for travelers to visit:

Roses Market (Mercat de Roses): This market in Roses provides a range of fresh vegetables, local items, and typical Catalan gastronomy. Fruits, vegetables, fish, cheeses, and other items are reasonably priced for visitors. It's a terrific spot to sample local cuisines and buy low-cost ingredients.

Tossa de Mar Municipal Market (Mercat Municipal de Tossa de Mar): This municipal market in Tossa de Mar has a variety of vendors offering fresh fruits, vegetables, meat, seafood, and other local items. The market is noted for its low costs and realistic shopping experience.

Sant Antoni de Calonge Market (Mercat de Sant Antoni de Calonge): Located in the village of Sant Antoni de Calonge, this market is popular with both residents and visitors. It sells fresh vegetables, handmade items, apparel, and accessories, among other things. Visitors may discover inexpensive things while enjoying the lively ambiance.

Market of Palafrugell (Mercat de Palafrugell):
Palafrugell is a lovely village on the Costa Brava that offers a weekly market. Visitors may peruse the booths, which offer local products, flowers, handicrafts, apparel, and household goods. Prices are normally inexpensive, making it an excellent choice for budget-conscious vacationers.

Blanes Market (Mercat de Blanes): Blanes is a picturesque seaside town famed for its botanical gardens and gorgeous beaches. Its market sells a wide variety of goods, including fresh fruits and vegetables, fish, spices, apparel, and other items. Tourists may get fantastic prices on local things while also enjoying the bustling scene.

Remember that market schedules sometimes change, so verify the opening days and hours before going. Furthermore, negotiating is uncommon in Spanish markets, but you may always hunt for the greatest offers and compare costs among various booths.

Chapter Nine

Goodbye, Costa Brava

Goodbye, Costa Brava, where golden sunsets kissed turquoise waters and memories were carved on the dunes. A location where laughter danced in the sea wind and time seemed to stand still among the craggy rocks.

Costa Brava Tourists Take Home Souvenirs

Costa Brava, situated in Catalonia's northeastern area, is recognized for its magnificent coastline, picturesque communities, and rich culture. There are various great alternatives for souvenirs to consider. Here are some of the most popular Costa Brava tourist souvenirs:

1: Ceramics & Pottery: Catalonia has a strong pottery culture, and Costa Brava boasts a wide selection of finely produced ceramic goods. Look for dishes, bowls, vases, and tiles with classic patterns and bright colors.

2: Local Wine: Costa Brava is located in the Empordà wine area, which is noted for producing high-quality wines.

Consider buying a bottle or two of local wines such as Empordà DO or Cava to enjoy the region's tastes at home.

3: Catalonia is also well-known for its olive oil production. Costa Brava produces high-quality olive oil from local olives. Look for extra virgin olive oil bottles, which make a delightful and healthful keepsake.

4: Cadaqués, a gorgeous Costa Brava beach town, is famous for its anchovies. The area is known for producing some of the best anchovies in the Mediterranean. Pick up a container of marinated anchovies or anchovy filets to eat as a snack or to use in your dishes.

5: Espardenyes (Espadrilles): Espadrilles are traditional jute and cloth shoes. In Costa Brava, you may discover a wide range of espadrilles, from basic to complex designs. These trendy and comfy shoes are a fashionable keepsake to carry home.

6: Handcrafted Jewelry: The Costa Brava region is home to many brilliant artists who produce one-of-a-kind jewelry.
7: Look for handcrafted earrings, necklaces, bracelets, or rings fashioned from local materials and patterns.

8: Local Art: Throughout the years, Costa Brava has inspired many artists, including prominent luminaries like Salvador Dal. Consider buying a poster or a small piece of artwork that symbolizes the region's creative legacy or captures its beauty.

9: Classic Catalan Sweets: Indulge in classic Catalan sweets such as panellets (marzipan-based pastries), (thin wafers), and xuixos (pastry rolls filled with cream). These delights make excellent keepsakes or presents for friends and family.

Remember to visit local markets, artisan shops, and specialty stores in Costa Brava to get one-of-a-kind and original items that represent the region's charm and culture.

Safety Tips for First-Time Visitors

If you're visiting Costa Brava, a lovely location in northern Spain for the first time, it's crucial to keep a few safety precautions in mind to guarantee a safe and happy vacation. Here are some suggestions:

- Plan ahead of time by researching the location, its attractions, and the regions you want to visit. Learn about local customs and traditions, as well as any special safety concerns. Planning ahead of time will allow you to make more informed judgments and prevent needless risks.

- Keep up to date on weather conditions: During your stay in Costa Brava, check the weather forecast on a regular basis. The area has a Mediterranean climate, however weather may vary quickly. Prepare for possible rainstorms, high temperatures, or strong winds, and modify your activities appropriately.

- Take sun protection: The Costa Brava receives a lot of sun, particularly in the summer. Wear sunscreen with a high SPF, a hat, sunglasses, and lightweight, breathable clothes to protect yourself from dangerous UV radiation. During the warmest hours of the day, stay hydrated and seek shade.

- Swim with caution: Costa Brava is noted for its stunning beaches and crystal-clear seas. Swimming is a popular hobby, but it is vital to use care. Always swim in specified areas where lifeguards are present, heed any posted warnings or flags, and be wary of strong currents or undertows. Consider donning a life jacket if you are not a competent swimmer.

- Water sports should be practiced safely: If you want to participate in watersports such as surfing, kayaking, or paddleboarding, be sure you have the essential abilities and expertise. Rent equipment from trusted vendors and observe all safety precautions. Check local restrictions and be mindful of any prohibited areas or dangerous currents.

- Keep an eye on your stuff: As with any tourist site, it's critical to keep a watch on your valuables to avoid theft. When possible, avoid carrying significant quantities of cash or precious objects. Keep your valuables near to you with a safe bag or money belt, particularly in busy places. Avoid leaving your valuables unsecured and be wary of pickpockets.

- Respect the environment: The Costa Brava has beautiful natural scenery and protected places. It is essential to respect the environment and adhere to any laws or regulations in existence. Stay on authorized trails, avoid littering, and be cautious of any animals you see. Contribute to the preservation of the region's attractiveness for future visitors.

- Use dependable transportation: When exploring Costa Brava, use dependable and licensed transportation alternatives. If you're renting a vehicle, get acquainted with local traffic laws and drive carefully. When in doubt, choose trustworthy taxi services or public transit, particularly if you're unfamiliar with the region.

- Keep in touch and informed: Make sure you have access to emergency contact numbers such as local police, medical services, and your embassy or consulate. To keep updated about any safety issues or developments throughout your journey, stay connected to credible sources of information, such as local news or travel advisories.

- Last but not least, follow your intuition and employ common sense. Remove yourself from a situation or region if you feel uncomfortable or dangerous. Pay alert to your surroundings, respect your personal space, and don't be afraid to seek help if necessary.

Remember that these are basic recommendations, and it is always best to tailor them to your unique situation. Have a wonderful time in Costa Brava!

Itinerary for 7 Days in Costa Brava

The length of time you should stay in Costa Brava as a tourist depends on your tastes and the activities you wish to participate in.

Here is an example schedule for a 7-day vacation to Costa Brava:

DAY ONE : Arrival in Barcelona, then transport to the Costa Brava.

Spend the day adjusting into your new surroundings and visiting the surrounding neighborhood.
Tossa de Mar is a charming village with ancient beauty and beautiful beaches.

DAY TWO; Visit Girona and the Dal Triangle

Exore Girona, a medieval city with a well-preserved old town and a stunning cathedral, for a day excursion.

In Figueres, visit the Dali Theatre-Museum, which is devoted to the famed surrealist artist Salvador Dal.

DAY THREE : Natural Park of Cadaqués and Cap de Creus

Explore Cadaqués, a lovely seaside town noted for its white buildings and artistic past.

Hike along picturesque pathways and enjoy spectacular views at the adjacent Cap de Creus Natural Park.

DAY FOUR: Explore the Beaches and Water Sports

Spend the day lounging on one of Costa Brava's magnificent beaches, such as Platja d'Aro, Lloret de Mar, or Begur.

Participate in watersports such as snorkeling, kayaking, or paddleboarding.

DAY FIVE: : Medieval Villages and the Wine Region of Empordà

Visit medieval villages like Pals and Peratallada, which are famed for their well-preserved architecture and narrow alleyways.
Explore the Empordà wine area, where you can enjoy wine tasting and local cuisine.

DAY SIX: Natural Parks and Outdoor Adventures

Discover the breathtaking scenery of Montgo Natural Park of Aiguamolls de l'Empordà Natural Park.
Participate in outdoor activities such as hiking, cycling, or horseback riding.

DAY SIX: Departure or Additional Exploration

Depending on when you leave, you may spend the morning relaxing on the beach or explore any remaining points of interest.

If you have extra time, you may prolong your vacation or return to Barcelona to explore more.

Remember, this is only a recommended schedule; you may change it to suit your tastes and the time you have available. Costa Brava has a lot to offer, from natural beauty to cultural attractions, making it a popular tourist destination.

Helpful Websites and Booking Resources

There are various helpful websites and booking services that may aid you in making plans and discovering relevant information while arranging a vacation to Costa Brava. Here are some suggestions:

Costa Brava Tourism Official Website: The Costa Brava Tourism Official Website gives detailed information on the area, including attractions, lodging, activities, and events. Their website may be found at *https://www.costabrava.org/en.*

Costa Brava lodging Booking.com is a prominent online platform that provides a large choice of Costa Brava lodgings. It makes it simple to compare costs, read reviews, and make reservations. ***Go to https://www.booking.com to*** learn more.

Airbnb: If you want to stay in private houses or flats, there are several possibilities in Costa Brava. You may locate distinctive and reasonably priced hotels that meet your needs. ***Visit https://www.airbnb.com*** to learn more.

TripAdvisor is a trustworthy website that offers reviews, suggestions, and travel information from other travelers. It includes Costa Brava hotels, restaurants, sights, and more. To learn more, go to https***://www.tripadvisor.com***.

Expedia is a well-known travel booking website that provides a variety of services such as flights, hotels, car rentals, and holiday packages. It can assist you in finding prices and planning your vacation to Costa Brava. Visit ***https://www.expedia.com*** for more information.

Facebook Costa Brava Groups: Joining Costa Brava-related Facebook groups may help you acquire suggestions, advice, and local insights from experienced tourists and locals. Find groups such as "Costa Brava Travel Tips" or "Costa Brava Travel Community" to connect with others.

Local Tourist Information Centers: Visit the local tourist information centers when you arrive in Costa Brava. Maps, brochures, and customized suggestions based on your interests are available from them. These facilities are often situated in the region's main towns and cities.

To make the most of your vacation to Costa Brava, remember to study and compare costs, read reviews, and plan your schedule ahead of time.

Conclusion

Finally, the Costa Brava Travel Guide encourages readers to embark on an extraordinary adventure through northeastern Spain's rocky and picturesque coastline. We have explored the different landscapes, rich history, lively culture, and gastronomic pleasures that make Costa Brava a wonderful destination throughout this handbook.

Costa Brava has something for everyone, from attractive fishing villages and pristine beaches to historic ruins and medieval towns. This guidebook has offered a detailed overview of the region's myriad assets, whether you want leisure on sun-kissed coasts, adventure in the untamed countryside, or absorption in the region's cultural and architectural legacy.

We have attempted to provide tourists with the tools they need to explore and enjoy the splendors of Costa Brava by providing practical suggestions and informative recommendations. We hope our choices have encouraged readers to design their own unforgettable itineraries, from touring the famed Salvador Dali Museum in Figueres to meandering through the cobblestone alleyways of ancient Girona.

Furthermore, we have honored the region's food, highlighting the necessity of appreciating and indulging in its delectable sensations. Costa Brava offers a gastronomic tapestry that will delight even the most discriminating palates, ranging from fresh seafood specialties to traditional Catalan meals.

While the natural beauty and historical sites of Costa Brava are undeniably appealing, the warmth and kindness of its inhabitants lend an added degree of pleasure to the encounter. Throughout our study of this region, we have met friendly residents eager to share their tales, customs, and hobbies, increasing our knowledge of the region's unique legacy.

As the voyage concludes, we invite readers to embrace the spirit of adventure and discovery, to step off the main road, and to immerse themselves in the myriad delights that Costa Brava has to offer. Costa Brava delivers an amazing vacation experience, whether it's exploring secret coves, hiking routes with stunning panoramas, or just experiencing the delight of slowing down and bathing in the Mediterranean ambience.

May this guide serve as a portal to the enchanted world of Costa Brava, a location where nature, history, culture, and food coexist to produce an unforgettable and treasured experience. We hope it encourages readers to go on their own personal trip along the enthralling coasts of this Mediterranean jewel, cultivating a strong connection with its beauty and leaving them with enduring memories of a really unique experience.

Made in United States
North Haven, CT
04 October 2023

42364695R00067